SPIRIT TEACHES A SIMPLE SEEKER

THE ART OF TIMELESS WISDOM

Book One

Jean Whitred

BALBOA.PRESS

A DIVISION OF HAY HOUSE

Balboa Press books may be ordered through booksellers or by contacting:

Balboa Press
A Division of Hay House
1663 Liberty Drive
Bloomington, IN 47403
www.balboapress.com
844-682-1282

Print information available on the last page.

ISBN: 978-1-9822-2867-5 (sc)
ISBN: 978-1-9822-2869-9 (hc)
ISBN: 978-1-9822-2868-2 (e)

Library of Congress Control Number: 2019906867

Balboa Press rev. date: 11/24/2020

Introduction:

How and when did I become a simple seeker? Perhaps I was born to be as I am or seem to be. And perhaps you, dear reader, were also born to be just as you are, beneath all the social conditioning that has influenced your thinking from the moment you were born, if not earlier.

We each learn how to live by living, and there may be no better way. Of course, we often, or not so often, mess up. So what? It may all be part of a lifetime learning experience.

I've always been so critical of myself, as if I expected myself to be perfect, even though that seemed impossible, for me. Spirit tells me that it's more than unhealthy; It's self-destructive to devalue ourselves. We can never be more than we are at any given time, He tells me, but we owe it to ourselves to become aware of both our weaknesses and our strengths, and to intend to improve.

It's all about love, He tells me. We are each and all loved more than we may ever know. Who loves us? Of course, we each love ourselves more and/or less, and some of us seem blessed to be loved by some others, but our unique inner spirit loves us with an unconditional love, just as we are.

Then, why try to understand life? For me, it's a personal journey that we each and all share, with or without awareness of life being a journey of discovery, and/or of moving along the road (or path) of Life.

I invite you all to share my experiences with Spirit as my guide and teacher, as if they were your own, and in some way, they are, or may be.

Jean

An Explanation of Spirit's Teaching Style:

Life lessons learned are as steps that move us along our path or journey through Life by teaching us to think and consider possible alternatives to each thought, emotion, or action that we choose to respond to the countless events, situations, and relationships we participate in during our activities of daily living.

The thirty-three lessons shared within this book are not to be considered as being sequential, random, nor alphabetical in importance. They each stand alone, and yet at the same time, are designed to contribute to the overall emotional, intellectual, and spiritual development of the seeker.

Spirit's style is to stimulate thinking, which has a higher priority than any of the thirty-three lessons, or topics of discussion, either singularly or collectively. Stimulation of thinking is as an end in itself, while the topics discussed contribute, if they do, to that end. Expansion of awareness can't possibly develop without an ever-expanding capacity to think.

Where does love fit into Spirit's educational method? Quality of thought, Spirit tells me, necessarily inspires quality of emotion, just as quality of emotion inspires quality of thought. Love and wisdom are in harmony with each other, or they're not what they may claim to be. It's as simple as that.

Jean

Contents

LESSON 1
A Beginning

A simple seeker was lost in thought. What thought? She was meditating on The Fool, the Tarot's anti-hero, or so he seems to be, at least as he begins his journey through Life. He isn't even given a number, unless zero can be considered as such. Like herself, or as she once was, he seems to be full of high hopes and self-confidence. But, again, as she once was.

"How are you any different, now?"

"I don't quite fit the picture anymore, if I ever did?"

"In what way?"

"The Fool, at the beginning of his journey, has no real-life experience and is totally unaware of immediate dangers, let alone of those that are waiting for him, somewhere down the line. He's lost in thought, enjoying the perfume of the rose that he's holding in his hand. He doesn't see the cliff that he's about to step off, into high altitude. Even his small, four-legged companion seems unable to warn him. But, perhaps we were all innocent at some time in our past."

"What would it look like?"

"The Fool, I guess."

"Yes, and yet, as the Tarot's Fool will discover through life experience, innocence is a beginning – the only possible beginning of our life's journey, our mission to discover who and what we each are."

"Only a beginning?"

"Yes, but an important one."

"In the sense that we have to start somewhere?"

"Yes, or something like that."

A simple seeker's note to herself

Lesson 1   Thinking back on my discussion with Spirit, what did I learn, if anything?

"Perhaps, I was trying to help you to understand that life experiences are as lessons. We learn something from everything that we experience, or we might."

"How can we know if we've learned from them?"

"We?"

"Okay, me. How can I know if I've learned from my life experiences?"

"Which life experiences?"

"Any of them."

"Perhaps you need to choose which life experiences need to be reflected or meditated upon, to protect yourself from repeating them, if they were unpleasant, and to find a way to repeat them if they seemed to be pleasing."

"To try and learn from my mistakes?"

"Yes, and to try to attract more of those experiences that seemed to have a positive outcome."

LESSON 2

A Common Root

A simple seeker was meditating on her spirit teacher's explanation of their relationship. He didn't need physical existence or human form, He told her.

"Why?"

"I use you as ballast, to connect to your particular world of illusion."

"If my world is one of illusion, and I can reluctantly accept that it is, or seems to be, at times, then at least some others must also be living in a personal world of illusion. Are they each separate from each other?"

"Yes. We each seem to know that our so-called individual world is intricately connected to everyone else's world, even though surface appearances deny this reality.

Only on the surface do our individual worlds of illusion appear to be separate. Beneath this illusion there's a common root that holds us together; that connects us inextricably together, as one."

A simple seeker's note to herself

Lesson 2   Perhaps Spirit was helping me to accept that we live in a world of illusion if we think that we're separate from other people, places, and things. But He and I live in different worlds.

"Worlds are as communities, and the same rules apply; the correspondences are the same. No world is totally isolated from any other. The forces, or universal laws of integration and synthesis impel us to develop personal relationships with other individuals and groups of individuals.

Perhaps, not-so-simple seeker, you also learned that there's no real separation between people, places, and things. Everything and everyone is connected to everything and everyone else. The ten thousand forms of plant life each contain roots that connect them to a common ground that nourishes them all, and without which they couldn't survive.

Collectively, we're as a picture puzzle, with each being as a piece of the whole. There is only one world, which contains all smaller worlds. There is only one humanity, which contains all races. There is only one religion, which contains all religions. We each may live in different ways and/or in different worlds, but we each live."

LESSON 3

A Dynamic Relationship

A simple seeker was meditating on the mystery of Tarot.

"How did you manage to move your focus from The Hermit, as a solitary seeker of enlightenment, to comparing Aces?"

"The Major Arcana, which includes The Hermit, relates to general personality characteristics, while…"

"Did I ask…?"

"The Aces introduce each of the four suits of the Minor Arcana, and offer a sacred gift – a promise, almost."

"How could a gift, or promise, be sacred and still be no more than an almost?"

"It's not a freebee."

"Then what does it cost?"

"It's not for sale; at least it can't be purchased."

"Then, how does one receive a gift that isn't free, and yet can't be purchased?"

"It's a promise of reward, if effort is made to follow one's dream, or path, and is meant to inspire self-confidence."

"How does Tarot differ from I Ching?"

"You're asking me?"

"Yes."

"From my limited understanding?"

"Yes."

"Okay. They have little or nothing in common."

"How so?"

"I Ching explains and supports social stability, within a system of generally accepted rules of order."

"And Tarot?"

"Tarot explains inner dimensions of personal experience; feelings, desires, needs, fears, and interests, and helps us to make sense of them, and to learn to blend them together; and more. It encourages us to believe in our individual values, and inspires us to reach for success and happiness."

"And I Ching does not?"

"Personal satisfaction and happiness don't seem to be high priorities, from an I Ching perspective."

"Then, why study both?"

"We seem to need both individual, and collective, general rules of order; but we also need personal, emotional satisfaction."

"Where does awareness fit into this two-sided view of the ideal society?"

"I didn't call it ideal."

"No. I did."

"Then, I'll let you explain where and how awareness fits into the picture."

"Awareness is understanding the reality that the individual and collective are as two parts of an infinite oneness, within which they share a dynamic relationship to each other."

A simple seeker's note to herself

Lesson 3   Spirit seemed to be helping me to understand that, though I live my individual life, I also live as a contributing member of a community.

"Yes, and this is necessarily so, even within our individual families and neighbourhoods."

"We can't escape being personally responsible, both for ourselves and others?"

"Why would you want to escape from responsibility?"

"It can get too much, when everyone seems to want from me something that I can't give, without giving less to myself."

"Perhaps the secret is to develop a sense of balance between caring for self and caring for others."

"That sounds easy enough, but how to live it in the real world of everyday interactions with others?"

"If you study both I Ching and Tarot, with intent to learn, you will discover how to balance your personal needs and desires with your responsibilities and/or duties to your family, your loved ones, and to the many levels of society that you necessarily are a part of. And then, having done what you can, release yourself from any further responsibility."

"Does it really work?"

"Yes, it really works if you work at it. Of course, you don't really need to study Tarot, I Ching, or any other formal, or less than formal system. You could simply learn to trust yourself to do what seems right in any given situation."

———◦◦◦———

LESSON 4

A Higher Infusion of Energy

A simple seeker was meditating on the concept of reverse transcendence.

"How did that idea get into your mind?"

"I don't know. Perhaps You put it there."

"For what purpose?"

"Perhaps to inform me of the topic of today's lesson."

"How would you explain reverse transcendence?"

"In traditional yoga practice, the mind of the student and that of her teacher become interconnected."

"Where does reverse transcendence fit into such a situation?"

"As the student absorbs more and more of her teacher's understanding…"

"Understanding? And not wisdom?"

"Are they not the same?"

"Yes. Go on."

"Then, her own wisdom, or awareness, expands as she absorbs some of his."

"Does she transcend her own mind?"

"No. An overlap, such as in a paradigm shift, develops between the student's mind and that of her teacher's."

"Duality becomes one?"

"Not totally."

"So, she absorbs his energy without losing her own?"

"Perhaps our unique energy could never be in danger of being consumed by another."

"It could be weakened or strengthened. Is this the result of a student attracting and absorbing her teacher's energy?"

"Perhaps neither happens."

"Then, what does, or might happen?"

"The student may become increasingly aware of her own vibrating energy, through a more relaxed and trusting association with his."

"Very good. But where does the concept of reverse transcendence come in?"

"I'm still vague about it, but transcendence suggests going beyond, and, if her guru's energy is strengthening her own, then the flow of higher energy is from without to within – a reverse flow from the generally accepted view of transcendence as going beyond, or from within to without."

"Does the teacher lose anything from this transfer of energy?"

"Is there a transfer?"

"Yes."

"Then the higher energy that the teacher transmits to his student would be replaced by an even higher infusion of energy from his source of enlightenment, as a pressure gradient system might work."

"Is that all?"

"For now, yes. Did I do well?"

"For now, yes."

A simple seeker's note to herself

Lesson 4   Thinking back on my discussion of transcendence with Spirit, what did I learn?

"Perhaps you learned that transcendence is not possible without an infusion of Higher Energy into your mind."

"Yes, but what triggers such an infusion of higher energy?"

"What triggers growth within your body?"

"My body may be designed to grow when nutrients are provided."

"Yes, and yet it grows from within to without."

"But it can only expand when nourished by outside forces."

"Yes, and so it is with your mind."

"Could you be considered as an outside force?"

"From the perspective of your limited mind, yes."

LESSON 5
Alone if Necessary

A simple seeker was meditating on the concept of serving a sacred cause, alone if necessary, but not necessarily alone.

"What cause?"

"I don't know."

"So, all that is missing is the cause?"

"The cause? Not, a cause?"

"Could it be any cause?"

"No."

"Then, that narrows the field, somewhat."

"You're mocking me."

"Yes."

"But I do seem to need to do something with my life."

"You have."

"What have I done?"

"You've lived."

"So has everyone else."

"Yes, but with a difference."

"And the difference is?"

"Everyone else lives his or her own life."

"And I have lived mine?"

"Yes."

"Bu; that relates to the past."

"Are you not living, now?"

"In the present?"

"Where else can you live, now?"

"I want to do something in the future that I haven't done in the past, or now."

"What?"

"I don't know."

"Will you know in the future?"

"Yes, of course, But i want to plan to do something."

"How you'll do, whatever you'll do?"

"How can I know how to do what, when I don't know what to do?"

"How have you done what you did in the past, and are doing now, in the present?"

"I did what I seemed to need to do, as well as I could."

"We can never do more than that."

A simple seeker's note to herself

Lesson 5   Thinking back on my discussion with Spirit about planning for the future, He seemed to be reminding me that we each live our life from day to day, more and/or less, and that it's just not possible to know for sure what will be important to us in the future. But, if we work to do what's important to us, now, as well as we can, then we'll be developing skills and habits which will help us adapt to whatever the future brings our way.

"Yes. Study and practice whatever you think is important for you to do now. In the future, perhaps you'll be interested in something else. So what? Then you can study and practice doing that something else. The skills you're learning now, and the study habits you're developing now, can be adapted to whatever situation and/or opportunity that presents itself in the future. You'll be prepared."

LESSON 6
A Map is a Guideline

A simple seeker was meditating on the concept of intention, and she was attempting to connect and merge individual human energies with those expressed on the Kabbalah Tree of Life, and, also necessarily, those expressed on the Ladder of Light. To be on one tree …

"Not on, but within."

"We're moving beyond form?"

"We were always beyond form."

"Then, what purpose does form serve?"

"As a map."

"Where does intention fit on the map?"

"Intention isn't on the map."

"But, if the map is a guide, …"

"A guideline; not a guide."

"But, the structure of the map …"

"Or tree, or ladder?"

"Yes. Don't they point a way to travel?"

"No."

"Then, what purpose do they serve?"

"They represent possibilities"

"Potential possibilities from which to choose?"

"Choose what?"

"The path, or way we want to travel, from among the various possibilities represented on the map."

"Yes. We choose the way we want to travel."

"As we go?"

"Where?"

"Along our way."

"Which way is our way?"

"The way we have chosen to travel."

"A predetermined way?"

"Can it be considered as a predetermined way if I'm only considering the next step?"

"Yes."

"How is that possible?"

"It's the only way."

"How can that be, if I see the destination that I wish to reach?"

"Wishing isn't moving."

"Then choosing…"

"Yes. If we consciously choose the destination that we wish to reach, if we can, then a map can provide us with a guideline."

"But intention is our guide along the way?"

"Yes."

A simple seeker's note to herself

Lesson 6   Looking at a map doesn't move us anywhere. We can sit in a café and study a map, and even make plans about where we'd like to go, but we have to get up on our feet and start moving, if we intend to get anywhere.

"Yes, looking at a map doesn't get us anywhere, but it does help us to plan where, how, and when we intend to go."

"But even then, we need intention to inspire us to move forward?"

"Or backward, up or down, this way or that way."

"Please explain."

"A map as a guideline can refer to a plan of moving forward with our life, in many more ways than one. A daily schedule is as a map of how we plan to spend our time."

"Are you suggesting that I need such a map?"

"Do you plan your daily activities?"

"For activities of importance, yes."

"What percentage of your daily activities are important enough for you to plan for?"

"I do prioritize. Isn't that planning?"

"Yes."

LESSON 7
A Materialized Adept

A simple seeker was accepting the reality of being something akin to being possessed, even though the very thought of that possibility sent shivers of fear through her body. It seemed to bring memories or stories; or were they from lived experiences of an earlier lifetime, of the torture inflicted upon millions of helpless individuals (mostly young women), who were accused of being witches, by self-proclaimed but generally accepted, male representatives of God.

Of course, Spirit may not be a spirit at all, but a materialized adept, living in a secret community, perhaps in the mountains of northern India, and using occult powers to control her, or attempt to; or attracted to her by the Universal Law of Attraction, to harmonize his wisdom with her simple thinking.

"What is a materialized adept?"

"A highly evolved spirit who has chosen a human disguise, in order to develop enlightenment among ordinary humans."

"So, a spirit in disguise as a human?"

"Yes."

"Aren't we all playing that game?"

A simple seeker's note to herself

Lesson 7   Thinking back to my discussion with Spirit about materialized adepts, if there are any, it might be as a game to Him, but for some of us, we may not be aware of being more than physical humans.

"Perhaps, for some, they're not yet aware of being much more than animals."

"Are we all materialized adepts?"

"Yes, and no."

"What does that mean?"

"What do you think it might mean?"

"That we're each and all spirit beings, living in a physical body."

"What about us all being adepts?"

"No. Perhaps a few of us might have that potential, but most of us are likely content just to live a physical life, within a wide variety of states of awareness."

"Yes, and, the problem arises of how to live in harmony with people who may possess different states of awareness, and a possibly infinite variety of personal rules of conduct toward other people."

"Strict, general rules of order would necessarily have to be designed to ensure peaceful co-existence."

"Yes, and if necessary, enforced."

"By whom?"

"By those who have power and/or a sense of responsibility to do so."

"How do they get that power?"

"Freely given or taken."

LESSON 8
And Anyone Else

The Page of Wands looked strangely familiar, and yet …
It was the image of a young boy, dressed up in clothes that he
didn't seem to feel comfortable wearing.

"What does it say to us?"

"It wouldn't say the same to me as it would to you."

"How do you know? Or, do you?"

"What does that mean?"

"When anything, or anyone, speaks to our inner knowing,
we're receiving a message, and we know it."

"Can it be an important message?"

"It's always more than important. It's vital to our self-
interest and to our personal world."

"That would create inner tension."

"Yes."

"Who wants inner tension?

"It's not a case of wanting.

"Then, needing?"

"Yes."

"Why do we need inner stress?"

"There's a difference between stress and tension.

"In degrees?"

"In cause. The situation causes tension, and…"

"Ignoring the message of tension causes stress?

"Yes."

"So, if we feel stressed, then it's not directly caused by the situation?"

'Exactly. Too many people seem to attempt to cope with stress with medication, instead of meditating on its possible cause, either alone or with a trusted and qualified teacher."

"Are we talking about you and me?"

"Yes, and anyone else who cares to listen."

———————>∞∞<———————

A simple seeker's note to herself

Lesson 8   Thinking back on lesson 8, what did I learn about tension and stress?

"You may have learned that tension is a necessary part of daily life."

"Things don't always go smoothly?"

"Exactly, and that's a blessing."

"How can tension be considered as a blessing?"

"Without tension, nothing can happen. Nothing can move. Nothing can get done. Nothing can grow or change"

"What causes tension?"

"Opposing forces."

"Such as?"

"The desire to learn more, to do more, and to become more than we now seem to be, and yet to fear change."

"Why do we fear change?"

"Change is as the unknown. We don't know what will be expected of us."

"By whom? Or what?"

"Perhaps, by ourselves."

"Lack of self-confidence can keep us stuck in old ways of doing, thinking, and being?"

"Yes."

LESSON 9
An Empty Mind

A simple seeker was meditating on her recent and strange discussion (if it could be called that) with Spirit.

"If it could be called what? A discussion? Strange? Or, a strange discussion?"

"I'm still trying to figure it all out, and any discussion with You has to be considered as strange, in that it's not a generally accepted possibility. Added to that was the topic of spiritual philosophy."

"Is spiritual philosophy also not generally considered to be possible?"

"No. On the contrary, spiritual philosophy is very much a part of New Age Thinking."

"What's New Age Thinking?"

"It's thinking about life, and what it is, and about how we can learn to live in harmony with each other, and with the environment."

"Hasn't that always been generally accepted?"

"Yes, perhaps, but New Age thinkers are not restricted to a specific school of thought, such as religious beliefs, or other exclusive group thinking, such as a particular scientific theory as having a final answer."

"A final answer to what?"

"To the origin or possible purpose of life, gender, relationships, potentials, truths…"

"So, where are you in all of this so-called new age spiritual philosophy thinking?"

"That's the beauty of it all. I don't have to be anywhere."

"Why?"

"My thinking can adapt and change as I'm introduced to new ideas. That's called being open-minded."

"How does your open mind differ from an empty one?"

"An open mind is open to continuously accepting new thoughts, and then, possibly trading them for even newer thoughts that seem to make more sense."

"And, an empty mind?"

"With an empty mind, no new thoughts are …"

"Why?"

"There's nothing in an empty mind to attract thoughts."

"No foundation?"

"Yes."

"Yes."

A simple seeker's note to herself

Lesson 9   Thinking back on our discussion about new age spiritual philosophy, I may have seemed a bit foolish to Spirit.

"How did you seem to yourself?"

"Upon reflection?"

"Yes."

"I now understand that we need to be careful before trading old ways and ideas for new ones.'

"Yes. Times change and we need to learn to adapt to changing circumstances, and yet accepting that the old ways and ideas seemed to have served us well, if they did, while they did. Sudden change can create chaos. Caution can protect us."

"So, to adapt to change without necessarily losing total faith in the past?"

"Yes. We can, if we will to, learn to see old issues from a newer perspective."

LESSON 10
And Still a Long Way to Go

A simple seeker was reading Alan Seale' s "Create a World That Works." "How can that be done?" she asked herself.

"It's being done."

"By whom?"

"By everyone."

"And everything?"

"Yes."

"How are we doing it?"

"Simply by being."

"Being what?"

"No what necessary."

"What does that mean?"

"What might it mean?"

"Is being the same as living."

"In what way?"

"Existing."

"How?"

"Just as we are."

"We?'

"All of us."

"No."

"Then, what?"

"We each of us exist."

"Separately?"

"No."

"Then, what's wrong with my using 'we'?"

"It suggests one way."

"Is there more than one way?"

"For what?"

"For each of us to exist."

"Yes, and no."

"Please explain."

"We each are as we each are, in a continuous process of becoming."

"Becoming what?"

"We can never become a what."

"Then, becoming whom?"

"We are now whom we are."

"Then, whom are we?"

"We each are we."

"One?"

"Yes."

A simple seeker's note to herself

Lesson 10   Thinking back on lesson 10, I must confess, if only to myself, that I still have a long way to go, when it comes to understanding life, and I'm still not sure that I understand what Spirit was teaching me.

"What don't you understand about life."
"What it's all about, and why?"
"The general picture, or your own individual life?"
"Both."
"One fits into the other."
"In what way?"
"In every possible way."
"Then, how should I live my individual life?"
"Your way."
"How can I know which way is my way?"
"Whatever way works to help you feel satisfied with how you live."

LESSON 11

An Open Line to Higher Help

A simple seeker was meditating and trying to clear her simple mind.

"If it's that simple, then what's the problem?"

'You seem intent on interrupting my thinking about not thinking."

"Did I win, again?"

"Yes. I forgot what it was that I was trying to forget."

"Then, we both win."

"It's not as simple as that."

"What's the problem?"

"I'm supposed to let go of thinking on my own."

"Who told you that nonsense?"

"Why would it be nonsense?"

"Because, it's impossible."

"Why?"

"When you, or anyone, sincerely meditates, then your sincerity attracts, as if it had put in a call to, Higher help."

"We each have an open line to Higher help?"

"Yes. It's a Law of Life."

~~~~~~~

A simple seeker's note to herself

Lesson 11   Thinking back on lesson 11, I wonder what an open line to higher help really means.

"It means what I said it means."

"Yes, but how does it work?"

"It's a reward for effort."

"Please explain."

"When we have a problem that we've trying to solve, no matter what kind of problem, if we do all that we can to solve it ourselves, and then just walk away from it, or do something else, then, suddenly, we may know the answer. We've prepared our mind to receive. We've opened the door between intellect and intuition, a higher level of understanding life's problem."

<hr />

LESSON 12
Another Hero Gone

A simple seeker was mourning for someone she had never met, at least not in person, during this lifetime. He was, to her, as a hero – a giant of a man. Even the trees around her hung heavy, as if to share her mood.

"We each come for a purpose, and when we've completed our chosen role…"

"I like that story, but…"

"It's more than a story. But…?'

"If it was time to go…?'

"And it was."

"Then why did he have to …?"

"Perhaps, that was part of the plan."

"Whose plan?"

"His."

'And we each…?"

"And we each…"

"Do some of us choose to be bombed?"

"Not everyone who is."

"Then, what …?"

"We each choose, if we've developed the capacity to choose."

"And, the rest of us…?

"A supporting cast of millions."

"What purpose…?"

"To learn to develop your capacity to choose."

"To choose what?"

"And where, when, how and why?"

"And who?"

"Yes."

A simple seeker's note to herself

Lesson 12   Thinking back on lesson 12, it still distresses me to think that some of us might actually choose to live a seemingly meaningless life, or one full of dangers.

"What kind of dangers?'
"Any kind."
Any is vague and general. Be specific."
"Why would someone choose to be trapped between warring armies, or between forest fires that seemed to be merging?"
"Is that where you are, now?"
"No. I was just using these scenarios as examples."
"Why?"
"Why not?"
"Why not dare to come a little closer to home?"
"What does that mean?"
"What might it mean?"
"My personal situation?"
"Yes."
"I'm not sure how to describe it."
"Try."
"Okay. Why would I have chosen to struggle with someone I can't see?"

"Perhaps you didn't trust your physical senses and wanted to bypass them. Would I have had the same effect on your mind if you could see me?"

"Perhaps not."

"Yes."

LESSON 13

Another Way to See the Tree

"Existence comes before essence. Who said that?"

"Likely an existentialist."

A simple seeker was aware that her spirit teacher didn't seem to approve of assigning names as credits. He kept reminding her that ideas come to us. We don't go to them, nor do we create them from nothing. But, then, what we do with them is our choice.

His position on this and on some other matters, she thought, might be as a gentle, or not so gentle, put-down of her tendency to hero-worship.

"We don't call our parents by their personal names."

"That's different."

"How?"

"Calling your parents Mother and Father, or more casually, Mom and Dad, is a cultural tradition, and perhaps a step toward learning to respect authority, and those who have earned it, one way or another. The Kabbalah has much in common with your own cultural traditions, in this respect.

The Tree of Life represents needed structure in our lives. We develop from the bottom up. The Tree helps us to focus on form before essence."

"Why?"

"The letter of the law must be accepted and respected before attempting to understand the spirit of whatever law."

"Even if whatever law seems to make no sense at all?"

"Yes."

"Why?"

"Laws represent order and, even if it's time to change a law, one must attempt to understand what purpose it might have served at an earlier time."

"Then. it should be accepted without necessarily approving of it?"

"Yes. Law, as form, is both structure and a foundation, while essence has potential to expand and deepen, after the form is acknowledged and then, perhaps, adapted to meet changing circumstances."

"I really am blessed to have you share your wisdom with me. But I've been developing some insights of my own; a deeper awareness of ..."

"Humility?"

A simple seeker's note to herself

Lesson 13   Perhaps, sometimes I do get too sure of the truth of my own ideas, and I may need to learn to accept that there may be many more ways than one to see and/or understand any situation and/or idea. But, how to learn to see from other perspectives?

"You might try listening with intent to understand."

"The problem with that advice is that I might decide that the other position has at least as much validity as my own."

"Yes."

"What does that mean?"

"It means that you might then be able to reach a compromise or synthesis with differing opinions or ideas."

"Yes. Thanks."

"For what?"

"For helping me to understand that differences are negotiable, or they might be."

"Yes."

LESSON 14
Are Bad Guys Necessary?

A simple seeker was meditating on a confusing dream of being lost in traffic and intensive construction, on her way to church, to celebrate a harvest festival.

She could hear the service begin. A loudspeaker was being used, and yet it didn't seem to cause her to wonder why, even though it had never been part of any previous experience.

"Perhaps, during a dream, we're unaware of any other previous experience."

"Then, why was I aware of where I was trying to go, to a church that I once attended?"

"Yes. There's always a blend of the reality that we're familiar with, and that which we are not."

"Anyway, I was lost."

"Were you alone?"

"No. I was lost with a friend. But I was not totally lost. I was aware of being close to our destination."

"But something was different with the landscape?"

"Yes. Traffic was incredibly intensive, as was the density of new buildings under construction."

"What happened next?"

"I was almost hit by an expensive-looking car attempting to make a left-hand turn at an intersection. It was chasing after another car that had now sped away. I must have crossed the street before the car shrieked to a stop, close to me. What did it mean?"

"What did what mean?"

"My dream."

"What makes you think that it meant anything?"

"I know that it meant something."

"How?"

"I experienced it."

"What did you experience?"

"The possibly bad guys were very polite."

"Would they have been polite to whomever they were chasing?"

"No. He'd likely be dead."

"But you were impressed by their behaviour toward you?"

"Yes. They were well-mannered and seemed sincere."

"And yet, they might be killers."

"Perhaps whomever they were chasing was the bad guy."

"Are bad guys necessary?"

"It's easier to think of conflicting sides as having opposite values."

"Yes."

A simple seeker's note to herself

Lesson 14   As Spirit seems to suggest, perhaps my ideas of good guys and bad guys are socially conditioned attitudes. And yet, as a society, we seem to need to develop values of right and wrong.

"How?"

"From lived experience, I guess. But, until we're old enough and experienced enough to determine right from wrong and/or good from bad, we seem to need guidance and limits to what is acceptable and what is not, for our own sake and for that of the community we live in."

"Yes, and that's how certain traditions develop over time and in different communities, with the elders of the community accepting responsibility for guiding younger bodies and/or minds to develop healthy attitudes and ways of living that seem to fit the needs of a particular society at a particular time."

"That makes sense, but why wouldn't the wise elders of all societies have a similar idea of what was right and what was wrong?"

"They did, as ancient writings of all societies show."

"If they were similar in the beginning, then how did they become so different, now?"

"They're not much different, even now, except on the surface. People are basically the same, all over the world. They each and all need to feel safe and loved."

LESSON 15
A Restless Spirit

"Simple seeker, what is it that you claim to be seeking?"

"Why do you say claim?"

"How sure are you of what you're seeking, if you're seeking anything that you don't already possess?"

"In which case…"

"Yes."

"Does it matter?"

"Yes. We should know what it is that we don't now possess, and yet seem to need to."

"Perhaps…"

"Yes. Anything we might wish to have can be categorized under one general heading…."

"Peace of mind?"

"Yes. And, to the question that you are almost ready to ask, the answer is yes. It is possible to possess peace of mind. Would you like it?"

"No."

"Yes, a restless spirit, after my own heart."

A simple seeker's note to herself

Lesson 15   Thinking back at lesson 15, what did I learn about peace of mind?

"Perhaps you learned something about your own personality."

"Such as?"

"Such as a seemingly predisposition toward conflict, or tension, as some might call disharmony."

"I seem to resist peace of mind?"

"Yes."

"Why would I resist peace of mind?"

"Yes, why do you."

"I do?"

"Yes."

"Perhaps…"

"Yes. We are energy beings and energy flows."

"And the comfort zone of each of us may be set at a unique level of motion?"

"Yes."

LESSON 16

Are You My Shadow?

A simple seeker was deeply engrossed in reading "The Shadow's Gift" by Robin Robertson, in which the author shares and discusses his personal experiences with psychic mediums, while maintaining an open mind as to their authenticity.

"What exactly would an open mind look like, in this instance?"

"Neither absolutely believing, nor absolutely disbelieving, but keenly interested in understanding exactly what was happening."

"Happening?"

"In terms of the subconscious activity of, or through, the channel or medium."

"What's the difference?"

"Between a channel and a medium?"

"Yes."

"Perhaps in essence, they're the same."

"Then, why did you mention both?"

"Are they not the same?"

"No."

"Then, what's the difference?"

"The difference is one of function."

"Please explain."

"A medium communicates between physical people and non-physical people."

"And, a channel?"

"She serves a non-physical person, or purpose."

"She?"

"Yes, you."

"Are you my shadow?"

"In a way, yes."

"What does that mean?"

"It means that we're each incomplete without the other."

"In what way?"

"I teach you, and you share my teaching with your blog readers."

"There aren't that many of them."

"There will be."

A simple seeker's note to herself

Lesson 16   Thinking back at lesson 16, what did I learn about psychic mediums and channels?

"Did you learn anything?"

"Yes."

"Then, what?"

"I learned that I seem to channel some of your teaching."

'How?"

"As a radio transceiver."

"What about a newscaster?"

"No."

"How do they differ?"

"I seem to assimilate the essence of what you share with, or teach me, but only as clearly as I can understand it. And then, I share it with my Facebook friends and the Facebook groups that I'm a member of."

"Do you know how many people pay any attention to what you post or comment?"

"No, but I'm learning so very much about life from you, and I enjoy sharing what you teach me with my Facebook community. Also, I'm gaining experience and learning from some posts and comments of others."

"Yes, it's a win-win situation."

LESSON 17

As Above –
So Below

A simple seeker was meditating on the concept of "as above – so below", and how it might express itself in human society.

"Is there a human society?"

"Perhaps the sum total of all human communities could be considered as an all-inclusive human society."

"Would the same principle …?"

"Is it a principle?"

"Its more than a principle. Its a law of Life.

"How many laws of Life are there?"

"There's no limit to their number."

"Is there a hierarchy within these rules of order?"

"Are they rules of order?"

"Are they?"

"Yes."

"Then …?"

"As above – so below."

"A common bond?

"Yes."

"What is the common bond?"

"Everyone possesses the same emotional and intellectual attributes as anyone else, but in varying degrees."

"Then why is there, or seems to be, an above and a below?"

"And a somewhere in between?"

"Yes."

"It's necessarily so."

"Why?"

"Birds of a feather flock together."

"Sparrows and crows don't associate with each other."

"Exactly. They each form their own societies, but are, at the same time, birds."

"The same species of life?"

"Yes."

"Then, what about the human species?"

"What about it?"

"Language groups."

"Yes, and separate cultures and communities develop within each language group."

"Is it possible to integrate all language groups and then to assimilate them into one?"

"Why would you want to? And, how would you do it without eliminating individual cultures?"

"Then, co-existence is the solution?"

"To what?"

"Co-existence is its own solution?"

"How to co-exist with others who are, or seem to be, superior or lesser to us, in some respects?"

"Between groups, or within groups?"

"The same principles would apply. The same laws of life apply."

"Those above know they're above, and those at the bottom…?"

"Yes."

A simple seeker's note to herself

Lesson 17   Thinking back on my discussion with Spirit about human and animal societies, what lesson of life was Spirit teaching me about similarities and correspondences between different species of life?

"What did you learn?"

"I learned that the same general laws, rules, or principles apply to all forms of life."

"Wrong."

"Wrong?"

"Yes."

"Please explain."

"As above, so below expresses some general correspondences between different levels of intelligence and/or life forms."

"Is there any correspondence or common bond between you and me?"

"Both. We each share an interest in clear and simple spiritual philosophy. That's the common bond."

"And the correspondence is that we each understand it at a different level?"

"Yes."

LESSON 18
A Simple Seeker Connects

A simple but sincere seeker of a higher level of spiritual development, somehow came under the influence of a spiritual guru whose understanding of life seemed to be...

"What do you mean by seemed to be?"

"Perhaps I don't yet know what the limits of my own understanding of life are."

"How is it possible not to know your own limits?"

"Perhaps I've been socially conditioned to accept and expect less of myself and my capacity for thought than possibly exists."

"Why would that have happened?"

"Not necessarily through the failure of anyone to teach me, unless..."

"Unless what?"

"Parents and early educators likely seek to serve the best interests of the community, when teaching children what to think and how to relate to their world."

"Wouldn't it be in the best interests of the community for children to be taught as much about life as they could understand?"

Perhaps the natural, or conditioned, limits of parents and early educators restricts what they can pass on to the younger generation in their care."

"Yes, but there is always conscious intent to limit awareness in the minds of young children."

"If so, that intentional limitation could have survival value."

"For whom? Or what? How? And why?"

"Perhaps it's as food."

"In what way?"

"We feed babies with very soft foods that their bodies can digest, and only gradually introduce foods that require a more developed digestive system."

"What has that to do with intentionally limiting a child's intellectual development?"

"Teachers and parents can only teach what they know."

"Or what they believe is safe for the children to know?"

"How could children be endangered by knowledge?"

"Perhaps not the children, themselves."

"Then whom? Or what?"

"Every society that exists can only maintain its present way of life by gently, or otherwise, enforcing rules on everyone within that society, including children."

"But, societies evolve and transcend, over time, as new ideas and new ways of living become available."

"Yes, but as eager as young people, and some others may be to adapt and change, there's always repression of adaptation and change, by those who might lose their positions of power within society."

"That could be a healthy condition."

"How so?"

"Survival needs of individual societies might depend upon at least some control by leaders, teachers, and parents, of the degree and type of change that seems to be happening."

"Yes. There are always reasons for suppression."

"Is it necessarily suppression?"

"What else?"

"Suppression sounds so deliberate and intentional."

"It is."

"Could it not just be resistance to change that might threaten the existing rules of order of the society in question?"

"Or the power of those who benefit from the current rules?"

"That, of course, would be part of any dynamic between the past and the desired future."

"Yes."

"So, what's the solution?"

"To what?"

"A peaceful transition from what was, to what yet might be."

"Yes, there is no peaceful solution."

"Winner takes all?"

"Yes."

A simple seeker's note to herself

Lesson 18   Thinking back at the concept of a "winner takes all" solution to any differences between either individuals or groups, is something that I've always resisted. I seem to need a level playing field kind of ending to any problems between people.

"Life doesn't usually work that way."

"Why?"

"Conflicting visions of an ideal society can create tension between the opposing views, unless both sides choose synthesis."

"Can't there be accommodation, cooperation, and harmony as an alternative to synthesis?"

"Perhaps, as a short-term solution, but it wouldn't last."

"Why?"

"It would still be duality."

"So, what's wrong with duality?"

"There's no unity in duality."

"Why do we need unity?"

"It's the only reality."

"What does that mean?"

"Either we're all in this together, or we're not, and we are. Case closed."

LESSON 19

A Simple Seeker Tries to Teach Spirit

A simple seeker decided it was time to teach her spirit guru about life in the world of physical reality.

"There is no physical reality."

"It looks pretty real to me."

"It's an illusion."

"As in a dream?"

"Yes, and no."

"Surely, it is, or it isn't."

"What?"

"A dream."

"It is, and it isn't."

"How can that be?"

"It is as a dream in that you are not directing it. But, the illusion of so-called reality allows you to pretend that you're directing it all."

"But I do make choices."

"Yes, from available options that you are aware of."

"How could I possibly choose from options that I wasn't aware of?"

"It's too late."

"For what?"

"It's too late for you to choose options that you might have, if you had been aware of them, when and while they were options."

"Then, how can there be any meaning to life?"

"There's always meaning to life."

"I mean, for me."

"Why are you living?"

"I don't know."

"Yes."

"What does that mean?"

"It means that you have yet to choose a purpose."

"How does one choose a purpose?"

"Which one?"

"This one. Me."

"Everyone chooses, every moment."

"How?"

"By living."

"Is living itself a purpose?"

"Yes."

"Then, we all have the same purpose?"

"Who?"

"Everyone living."

"Yes, and no."

"It only begins with living?"

"No."

"Please explain."

"There was no beginning."

A simple seeker's note to herself

Lesson 19   Thinking back at lesson 19, I wonder why I was trying to teach Spirit anything. I should have known that I'd lose. What was I trying to teach him, anyway?

"About life in the so-called world of physical reality?"

'If physical reality is an illusion...'

"And it is."

"Then, what purpose does it serve?"

"Does it serve a purpose?"

"Does it?"

"Yes."

"Then, what?"

"Physical experiences provide opportunities to develop skills, and practice understanding our interrelatedness with all other life forms."

"What purpose does understanding have?"

"It determines how we interact with each other; how we choose to interact with each other. But, choosing is only a step toward understanding."

"Understanding what?"

"Understanding that we are one."

———◦◦◦———

LESSON 20

Awareness as an Option

A simple seeker was meditating on the four Tarot Queens, until her mind seemed to rest or focus on The Queen of Cups.

"What about her?"

"I seem to relate to her."

"How?"

"Her throne has a high back, as does my new patio recliner, except that she looks much more at ease than I feel in this high-backed and oversized (for me) chair.

"Perhaps elegance has always been part of her life. Is hers the style to which you would like to become accustomed?"

"No. It's too late."

"It was always too late."

"Why is that?"

"We each have a path prepared for us."

"Isn't that fatalism?"

"No; destiny."

"What's the difference?"

"Fate is imposed from outside sources, or forces."

"And destiny is not?"

"Yes. Destiny is not."

"The acorn theory?"

"It's more than a theory."

"How would the results be different?"

"Fate allows for no adaptation to the journey or destination."

"And destiny does?"

"Yes."

"How"

"An acorn is destined to become an oak tree, but not all oak trees live to maturity, or grow straight and strong."

"Outside forces influence but do not determine the outcome?"

"Yes. A seed's inner essence determines the path it will follow. It knows what it is, where it's going, and why." Whether it arrives or not is out of its hands, and not worth considering."

"Then, why can't I be as an acorn?"

"You are. Everyone is."

"Whether they're aware of that reality or not?"

"Yes. Awareness is an option."

A simple seeker's note to herself

Lesson 20   Awareness as an option

"What did you learn, chela?"

"That we each are as a seed."

"In what way?"

"We each have unique strengths, weaknesses, and potentials, and each to variable degrees."

"Yes. So, how can that awareness help you choose how to live."

"By meditating on my personal strengths, weaknesses, and possible potentials, and, perhaps even more importantly, on those emotions, thoughts, and activities that I seem to be naturally attracted to."

"Yes. It all begins with learning to know yourself."

"Is that possible?"

"Yes, if only to some extent, and the rest is a mystery, for now."

LESSON 21

Awareness of Personal Power

A simple seeker had randomly chosen and was now studying, her daily, personal relationship Tarot card, The King of Wands. This authority figure presented as having a firm grip on power.

"Is it possible?"

"Is what possible?"

"To possess a firm grip on authority."

"He seems ready to do battle to maintain it. Beneath his royal robes, he wears a body suit of armour.

"Then he rules with an iron grip?"

"Wands are wood, but he does seem prepared, and yet…"

"And yet?"

"Something in his posture and facial expression suggest a willingness to listen to reason."

"Does he remind you of me?"

"Not at all."

"Why?"

"Wands express action."

"And teachers don't?"

"Not in a physical sense."

"Intellectual development has physical results."

"How?"

"Everything you do, say, or think is an expression of intellectual development."

"Wow!"

"Does that mean you agree?"

"No."

"Then, what?"

"It means that I'm impressed with your self-confidence."

"Yes, but do you disagree?"

"No."

"Why not?"

"Self-directed actions must be based on thoughts blended with emotions. And, our thoughts are influenced by those whom we have chosen, or have been chosen for us, to develop and guide our thinking."

"Do I guide your thinking?"

"Yes. You certainly have had a powerful effect on my thinking."

"In what way?"

"You have continuously, or so it seems, challenged me to defend or question my own thinking."

"And the effects of earlier teachers and social conditioning on your thinking?"

"Yes."

"Now, back to The King of Action."

"What about him?"

"I'll ask you, again. Do teachers possess power to influence their students' actions; what they say and do?"

"Yes, both now and in the future. I now understand the power of what we know, or think we know."

"Yes. We have learned from whomever we have allowed to teach us whatever."

"Is Free will involved?"

"Yes. For those of us who have developed awareness of being influenced by some others, we're each personally responsible for what we choose to learn from them."

"What about emotions."

"Have I taught you any?"

"How can anyone learn or teach emotions?"

"Nothing we can say, think, or do, is or can be emotion-free."

"How can we learn to recognize which emotion is embedded in whatever particular thought, word, or action?"

"Self-awareness."

"How to develop self-awareness?"

"Self-reflection, and meditation, in some form."

"How does self-awareness relate to the symbolic form of the King of Action?"

"His seeming sense of power is as a reflection of his self-awareness. He's aware of his own personal strengths; his personal power. Are you, of yours?"

"No."

"Yes."

A simple seeker's note to herself

Lesson 21   I wonder if Spirit was speaking about me when He said that "We've learned from whomever we've allowed to teach us whatever."

"You chose to listen to me. Why?"

"I seemed to intuitively know that I'd be wiser for listening to you."

"With intent to learn whatever I might teach you?"

"No."

"Then, what?"

"With intent to seriously consider whatever you might choose to share with me."

"Yes, and that's why I choose to share with you, what I do."

LESSON 22
Beauty and Evil

A simple seeker was meditating on something that St. Augustine was supposed to have said - that all evil has a reason.

"You seem to have difficulty accepting that reality, chela?"

"Reason sounds so overly deliberate and intentional."

"Is there a difference?"

"Intention sounds predetermined."

"And, deliberate?"

"Perhaps in the heat of the moment."

"As a reaction, rather than as a response?"

"Yes."

"And, intentional?"

"Either way, it would have to have had a pre-existing cause?"

"Yes."

"But a cause is not a justification, but just something that came before."

"Wrong."

"Wrong?"

"Wrong."

"Please explain."

"The number two comes before three, in simple number progression, but it doesn't cause three."

"Three is just the next number following two?"

"Yes."

"What has that to do with evil?"

"Everything."

"How?"

"Evil is a consciously, intentional, and extreme form of violence."

"That explanation seems to separate the evil deed from the doer of the evil deed."

"One is not the other."

"One who bakes is considered to be a baker."

"Regardless of the quality of her baking?"

"Doers of evil are not all the same?"

"Exactly. And, what is seen in the eyes of some as evil, may be considered by others to be a necessary or expedient means to further an end that may, or may not, in itself, be considered to be evil."

"The means doesn't necessarily measure the quality or value of the end result?"

"Yes."

"That's a sad situation."

"Yes."

A simple seeker's note to herself

Lesson 22   Thinking back at lesson 22, I don't feel comfortable with the idea that "all evil has a reason" even if St. Augustine said it; if he did.

"What's your problem?"

"If all evil…"

"Yes, and all good."

"But, some might do good because it's in their nature to do good."

"Yes, but they've developed that inclination or intention, over time."

"So, couldn't a doer of evil …?"

"No."

"Why?"

"Doers of evil haven't yet learned that evil doesn't pay. They'll suffer personally from their evil deeds more than any they harm, until they develop a higher level of consciousness."

"And they will?"

"And they will."

LESSON 23

Choosing Doesn't Create Value

A simple seeker of enlightenment was meditating on the Tarot's Eight of Cups and comparing different interpretations. But her emotional response was always the same; a sense of distress and excitement, at one and the same time, or of one mood rapidly replacing the other, in her mind. Why?

"Are you asking me?"

"No. I was thinking to myself, but according to some, it's the same thing."

"Is it?"

"No. I would know."

"What does it mean to know?"

"I would have had experience and I would have learned from it."

"Perhaps you have."

"Regarding choosing change rather than letting it choose me?"

"Yes."

"But I never choose lightly."

"The choice would have no value if you did."

"But, does choosing necessarily create value?"

"That depends."

"On what?"

"On how much is at stake in the choice."

"How can we know, for sure?"

"There is no knowing for sure."

"But the choice must still be made?"

"The choice has been made, in your mind, whether or not you dare to act on it."

"Yes."

"What does that mean?"

"You know that it means that I accept that you're right, again."

"Will that knowing determine your choice?"

"No."

"Yes."

A simple seeker's note to herself

Lesson 23   Thinking back at Lesson 23, did I learn anything about choosing and values?

"Can there be choosing without weighing values?"

"How important is one option compared to another?"

"Yes. Values have a difference in weight."

"How so?"

"Some are more lightly chosen and discarded."

"Yes, but there are also times when we must choose between two or more options of seemingly equal value. We can't go down two different roads, at the same time."

"Yes. Which path have you chosen, for life?"

"You know that I've chosen to follow you."

"Yes. We made a sacred vow, a long time ago."

———————◦◦◦◦◦———————

LESSON 24

Choosing Integrity

A simple seeker was meditating on the concept of wisdom.

"Wisdom is much more than a concept."

"How can anything be more than a concept?"

"How can anything be less?"

"Then, what is wisdom, beyond being a concept?"

"A concept of what?"

"A high level of understanding."

"Understanding of what?"

"Whatever."

"Whatever is a generalization of everything."

"Then, of life."

"Whose life? Or, what life?"

"Wisdom as a concept of life in general."

"Wisdom is wisdom, and life is life."

"Yes, but I want to understand what life is."

"How would wisdom help you do that?"

"I don't know."

"Perhaps you know more than you're willing to accept knowing."

"Why would I resist accepting knowing?"

"For fear of consequences of knowing whatever."

"What consequences can knowledge have?"

"Personal responsibility."

"For what?"

"For how you choose to respond to awareness."

"We were discussing knowledge."

"True knowledge is awareness."

"And, awareness is knowing?"

"Yes."

"Then, how to respond?"

"To what?"

"Knowing."

"With integrity."

"It could be risky."

"Yes."

A simple seeker's note to herself

Lesson 24   Thinking back at lesson 24, what did I learn about integrity? And, how did my discussion with Spirit about wisdom develop into one about integrity? He seems to have a habit of moving from one subject to another, or are they related?

"Perhaps you learned to accept that you know, or might know, more than you feel comfortable knowing."

"About what?"

"Or who?"

"Who?"

"You."

"I thought we were discussing the topic in general."

"What topic?"

"Wisdom."

"And integrity?"

"You slipped integrity into it."

"I'm allowed. I gave myself permission."

"Even so, we were speaking of generalities."

"The specific is the general."

LESSON 25

Choosing to do Nothing

A simple seeker was relaxing, or at least trying to, in her new patio recliner that seemed many times too big for her to feel comfortable in, just yet. It reminded her of the children's story of three bears and a young intruder.

But, today was a glorious day, in spite of, or perhaps because of, feeling dry and yet breathing in moist air, and taking pleasure in the one thousand and more shades of dripping green leaves, weighted down by the soft but steadily falling rain, just beyond her partially protected patio.

The raindrops seemed to slide from some leaves more willingly than from some others. Why?

"For many more reasons than one, perhaps."

"How can that be?"

"Shape, texture, angle of incline, location…"

"Yes. Some are more exposed to …"

"A direct hit?"

"That would suggest that the rain was attacking"

"And a victim mentality?"

"Where are you going with that?"

"Cause and effect is simply a sequential order of events."

"My lost tooth?"

"It wasn't lost."

"Why did you let it fall out?"

"It was ready to go. No need to blame me."

"But you could have prevented it."

"Why would I interfere with Nature?"

"I do it all the time, in my garden."

"You interfere with Nature's way?"

"Only when her way differs from mine."

"Why?"

"It's my garden."

"And, it's your tooth."

"But I couldn't save it without your help."

"And I have nothing better to do with my energy than to interfere with Nature, in such a small and inconsequential situation?"

"It isn't small, for me."

"Was it a large tooth?"

"You know it was small."

"And so was the issue."

"What lesson could I learn from your behaviour?"

"What did I do?"

"Nothing."

"Yes."

A simple seeker's note to herself

Lesson 25   Thinking back at lesson 25, why did I seem to think that Spirit would protect me from losing a tooth? I seemed to need and/or expect a more personal relationship with Him, and not just a teacher-student one.

"Why did you want a personal relationship with me."

"We would have been, or might have become, friends."

"And a friendly teacher would have protected you from experiencing what most everyone else experiences as they grow older?"

"Perhaps I'm too simple to understand why all relationships can't be mutually supportive."

"All healthy relationships are mutually supportive."

"Then, why did you seem so …?"

"I support your best interests more than you do, yourself."

"How?"

"By helping you to understand the difference between what is important and what is not."

"And my tooth was not?"

"Yes. Your tooth was not."

LESSON 26

Compassion Has a History

A simple seeker was practicing slow and deep breathing, to calm her over-charged emotions, after reading a passionate post of a patriotic soul, concerning her homeland, or at least the land of her birth.

The young journalist (did it require youth to care so deeply?) was obviously very agitated by what had happened, was now happening, and what might yet happen; all of it seemingly beyond her power to control.

"How did her energy affect your own, in such a way?"

"I don't know how that was possible. Perhaps we're kindred spirits."

"Yes. We each resonate at a frequency which magnetically attracts and resonates with others resonating with the same or a similar vibration."

"Through a computer?"

"No."

"Then how?"

"Thoughts have power to resonate, whether written, spoken, or reflected upon in one's own mind."

"Then, a computer…"

"Or a book…"

"I'm not going there."

"Where?"

"You've hinted at a book for the past ten thousand years or more. I don't care any more."

"Why?"

"I allowed myself to get too personally involved in the project."

"Yes."

"What does that mean?"

"It's the same with the young journalist, who has become a deeply distressed witness to a human tragedy."

"Expanded awareness would have allowed her to transfer her agitated emotions to empathy?"

"Yes, and then to compassion."

"Yes, and you're right, again."

"In what way?"

In that she seems to see her world too close up to allow for expanded awareness."

"Would she care less for current events if she could distance herself from them?"

"No. She would still know that she is helpless to change what is."

"What can she change?"

"I'm not sure."

"We can each change how we choose to respond to whatever situation."

"Would she have expressed less care if she had not shared her experience; her story?"

"Yes."

A simple seeker's note to herself

Lesson 26   I did seem to let myself get very emotionally distressed when reading about a human tragedy so very far away from the safety of my own little home.

"What did you learn, if you learned anything, from our discussion of the young reporter's experience, and her response to it?"

"I learned that we can't live anyone's life but our own."

"Yes, but you must have learned something more."

"What?"

"What did the young writer do?"

"She shared her experience?"

"Yes, and in the sharing, what she witnessed became the awareness of all who read her report."

"Her response to her experience?"

"Yes. We may be limited in our capacity to change the world, alone. But, if we share what we know, then we also share the responsibility of responding, with everyone with whom we share our story."

————⟷————

LESSON 27
Deep Breathing

A simple seeker was enjoying, or might have been enjoying, a glorious summer afternoon on her precious patio. A late-blooming bluish-purple clematis was stretching as open as it could go – seemingly determined to absorb as much as it could of the gently moving air. It seemed to sense, as did the lavender, which was also blooming longer than usual, that their time was running out, at least for this season.

A second blooming, or was it a third? of pink and yellow – a name; how could she forget the name? But, of course, she had not. It had simply slipped away, for now. However, the beautiful snapdragon blossoms had not slipped away, yet. Fuchsias and geraniums seemed also to know that these lazy days of summer were coming to an end.

The light-filtered green canopy above her would soon dry to glorious reds and golds. The leaves would flutter down, or be torn away and blown away, by the wind.

It was inevitable. Nothing could change what destiny had planned, and what fate seemed only too willing to help bring about.

"Aren't we getting a bit morbid?"

"But it's going to happen, and nothing can prevent it."

"Why would you want to prevent Nature from doing what Nature does every year at this time?"

"The slow dance of light and shadow is as silent music that the eye alone can hear. And the perfume of the gently moving air feels so good to inhale, that deep breathing is more as a delicious indulgence than a required meditation practice. It seems to connect me to, and within, this precious setting."

"Then, why are you sad?"

"It isn't enough to have it now. I want to experience it tomorrow, and next week, and … It's such a helpless feeling."

"Do your loved plants share your sorrow?"

"No. They seem to have accepted whatever will be, and are happy to be enjoying what now is, a glorious afternoon."

"What lesson could they teach you, if you were willing to learn it?"

"To enjoy what we have, while we have it, even while accepting that it isn't ours, forever."

"Yes. Not only is it not ours, forever, as far as this pleasant weather is concerned; it may be gone, tomorrow."

"Are you predicting stormy weather?"

"There will always be stormy weather, somewhere."

A simple seeker's note to herself.

Lesson 27   Thinking back at lesson 27, Spirit said that there would always be stormy weather, somewhere. What did He mean by that? I wonder if He was speaking of something other than nature.

"There isn't anything other than Nature."

"Yes, perhaps, but in this particular case, were you referring to physical nature or stormy states of consciousness?"

"Are there stormy states of consciousness?"

"Are there?"

"Yes."

"Do we each have stormy states in our personal consciousness?"

"There is no individual consciousness."

"Then, we each and all share the same consciousness?"

"Yes, and no."

"Please explain."

"We create the illusion of separate states of consciousness when, in reality, there are an infinite number of depths and qualities of consciousness that we each and all are a part of, and if we are stressed, then the Law of Attraction can supply us with ever-increasing quantities and qualities of that, or those thoughts or emotions that we focus our attention on."

"I let myself get pulled into negative thoughts re the changing season?"

'Yes. Your distress didn't change the weather, but it prevented you from fully enjoying the beautiful weather, while it lasted."

"Yes."

LESSON 28
Differentiation vs Separation

A simple seeker was meditating on the concept of separation, and how it might differ from differentiation.

"What seems to be the problem?"

"Seems to be, or is?"

"Seems to be, in the minds of some."

"In the minds of some?"

"Yes."

"But not in all?"

"Not in all."

"But; if all minds are individual aspects of the one..."

"And, they are."

"Then..."

"Go on."

"How can they be separate?"

"They can't."

"How is this possible?"

"Different meals can be prepared from the same ingredients. Apples are apples, whether they're served as a pie, or as a sauce."

"Or a drink?"

"Yes."

"But; different minds have varying degrees of potential."

"Not all apples are the same."

"So, differentiation could refer to various specific types of apples?"

"Or minds."

"How can a mind be a type?"

"We each possess potentials that some others may or may not possess."

"So, a mind is a mind, whatever its capacity or style of learning?"

"Style of learning?"

"Yes."

"Exactly. We each learn in our own way."

"But we each learn?"

"Yes."

"Then, our individual learning style doesn't necessarily separate us from others, who each learn at their own pace and in their own way?"

"Yes. We may be, in some respects, different in our habits, but we each develop habits."

"So, different individual habits, or even group habits, or social customs, don't necessarily separate these individuals or groups from each other?"

"Yes. We each and all share more similarities than differences."

A simple seeker's note to herself

Lesson 28   Thinking back at lesson 28, I wonder if Spirit was suggesting…

"It was more than a suggestion."

"Trees are trees, regardless of their type?"

"Yes, and people are people, regardless of their age, gender, strength, size, race, beliefs, education, skills, and special talents (or lack of)."

"So, our differences don't necessarily separate us from each other, unless we choose to let it happen, for whatever reason?"

"Yes, and in some instances, there can be very justifiable and/or good reasons for separating people, places, and things into categories. We don't usually put young children into the same school class with older students. It's mutually beneficial to teach younger students with others of their own general age and/or mental capacity."

"How does this discussion of differences and separation relate to you and me?"

"In what way?"

"We seem to be so different in levels of awareness, and yet we manage to relate to each other. How can that be?"

"We've each intentionally developed a style, a practice of recognizing our differences, and seeking to benefit from them."

"Would it work for others?"

"It's the only way that will work."

LESSON 29

Ego as Our Life Force

A simple seeker was meditating on a card she had pulled randomly from her Tarot deck, a lone figure with a lantern.

"Do you know what lived experience The Hermit card expresses?"

I seem to relate to it."

"In what way?"

"As a solitary seeker."

"How can you consider yourself to be solitary while I'm part of your life?"

"It's possible to be alone in a crowd."

"We're not a crowd."

"What difference does it make?"

"To what?"

"Aloneness in thought."

"What about aloneness in emotion?"

"What about it?"

"If you can feel alone in thought…"

You slipped "feel" in."

Yes, to prove a point."

"That thoughts aren't isolated from emotions?"

"Yes. They each are as one of two sides of the same reality."

"The reality of…"

"Our state of mind."

"I sense ego coming into the picture."

"Yes. Ego is the central mover and pusher of our thoughts, emotions, and actions. We can't do or even feel anything without our individual life force – ego."

"There may be thousands, and perhaps, tens of thousands of people who don't seem to be aware of this reality."

"This" suggests that you're aware."

"Yes, but I have no power of persuasion to inspire others to shake off the illusion of ego as being something they can function without, and still be able to live in the physical world as an individual, beyond the control of some guru more aware than they are."

"Yes. They'd be as slaves."

"Perhaps they are, now."

"Yes."

———————⟫∘∘⟪———————

A simple seeker's note to herself

Lesson 29   A sudden thought re the Hermit. Spirit may have caused my hand to pull that card.

"Why?"

"To help me understand that we each move through life alone, at least in some way."

"In what way?"

"Nobody can live our life for us."

"Personal responsibility?"

"Yes. It's unavoidable, I guess."

"Yes."

LESSON 30

Emptiness is Never Empty

A simple seeker was meditating on the concept of emptiness.

"What would it look like?"

"It wouldn't look like anything."

"What do you think emptiness means to a spiritual seeker, such as yourself?"

"Without form."

"What is without form?"

"Potential."

"What potential?"

"Any and all."

"Where does this emptiness, which is potential, exist?"

"Perhaps wherever there's no form."

"Where is there no form?"

"You're leading me somewhere."

"Where might I be leading you?"

"To asking you to please explain what it's all about."

"Yes."

"Please explain."

"What?"

"Where emptiness is, and what it might look like if I could recognize it."

"Emptiness and nothingness are never empty nor nothing. They are potential, as is everything and everyone."

"Then, we each have a never-ending potential?"

"To what?"

"To be and do."

"To be and do what?"

"To become."

"To become what?"

"More aware."

"Of what?"

"Of a slippery slope of enquiry."

"Yes."

A simple seeker's note to herself

Lesson 30   I'm beginning to become more aware of sometimes being pulled into a discussion with Spirit, and perhaps with some others, that's over my head.

"Of what?"

"Of everything."

"How is that possible?"

"How might it be possible?"

"With practice."

"Yes, and with intent."

"Intent?"

"Yes, with intent to become more aware."

"Aware of what?"

"Of why things seem to be the way they seem to be."

"What things."

"Relationships between people, places, and things."

"Yes."

"The problem is that it could require more mental energy than I possess."

"Mental muscles, as do physical muscles, develop with use."

LESSON 31

Evolutionary Buddhism

A simple seeker was puzzled by the seemingly contradictory and mutually exclusive (from her albeit limited understanding) terms of evolutionary and Buddhism rolled in together, in something she had been reading.

"What seems to be the problem?"

"Buddhism and evolution together?"

"Everything is together."

"But; spirituality should be forever."

"It is."

"But, not necessarily as it was or might yet be?"

"Exactly."

"Then, how can anyone…"

"Which anyone?"

"This anyone. Me. How can I hope to ever understand something that keeps developing; when it isn't what it once was, and, in the future, may not be what it is, now. I need stability."

"There isn't any."

"Then, what is there to hold onto?"

"In what way?"

"In thinking."

"You could try holding on to the concept of endless change."

"That would be easy if I was looking out from a high window at traffic below."

"We are doing just that."

A simple seeker's note to herself

Lesson 31   Thinking back on lesson 31, I wonder what Spirit meant by saying that we're looking down from a high window?"

"Whether we're looking down or back, it's the same. Distance allows for a wider perspective than does a close-up view. Evolution is change, and everything, including all relationships, and all situations, evolve.

Buddhism is not as it once was, nor as it might yet become. And yet, it has been, is now, and, in spite of possible future changes or adaptations, may still be Buddhism, without necessarily losing any of its original value.

We dress differently than our distant ancestors dressed, and even now we dress differently for different weather conditions or social events, and yet we still dress, more and/ or less."

"So, the lesson is to try to see beyond form?"

"Yes."

LESSON 32

Experience as a Teacher

A simple seeker was admiring, in her mind (but where else could she admire anything?), a beautiful pink rose that someone had generously shared on Twitter. But, as beautiful as the flower was, something else was going on. Envy was slipping into the picture.

"What's wrong with envy?"

"I want to be able to appreciate the skills of others without always wishing that I also possessed them."

"Do you envy everyone's skills?"

"No. Just those that I wish I also possessed."

"Why don't you possess the skills you admire?"

"Some people have more natural talent than do some others."

"Some people may be unaware of what so-called natural talents they do possess."

It isn't possible for me to develop all of the talents that I admire in other people."

"Have you tried?"

"There would never be enough time for that, and ."

"Yes. It would pull you away from what you are now doing well, or might, with a little more effort."

"How would that protect me from envy?"

"Nothing can protect you from envy."

"Why?"

"Envy, in its most sincere form, is a recognition of, and an inspiration toward, excellence. We each, at least to some extent, aspire toward higher levels of personal skills. Envy is seeing in others what we want for ourselves. It can encourage us."

"Or discourage us?"

"No. An unhealthy mind would feel resentment, not discouragement."

"How can we know the difference?

"Experience teaches us. We know because we've experienced it, if we have."

"And, if we haven't?

"Then, we will, sooner or later."

———⟞⟨∘∘∘⟩⟝———

A simple seeker's note to herself

Lesson 32   Thinking back at lesson 32, if experience is as a teacher, then what did my envy of the beautiful rose teach me?

"Perhaps you learned that we can't have it both ways. You may have wished that you could provide roses with what they need plenty of, sunshine. And, yet, you seem to feel more comfortable in shade."

"Yes, even my little garden areas are too shady for roses to survive in, let alone thrive in."

"We need to learn to accept what is and what is not possible with what we have. But; we can admire and even envy what others have, without wishing to change our life situation with theirs."

"Yes. I very much enjoy my little shady patio, and even my small and shady garden areas. I'd like more sunlight for them, and yet the trees are so beautiful. Perhaps I need to learn to appreciate more than I do, what I have. My plants do their best to adapt to what I can offer them. Let others grow roses, and I'll try to admire them without feeling too envious."

"A good idea."

LESSON 33

Feminism and Ancient Wisdom

A simple seeker was deeply engrossed in reading Tera Kathryn Collin's "The Three Sisters of Tao.'

"It's possible to read with much less intensity."

"Perhaps, for some, if what they're reading is for casual entertainment."

"Even some serious students allow themselves some distance from the text."

"Yes, it is as a text, with an important difference."

"And, the difference is…?"

"Personal experience."

"How can you be sure?"

"My own personal experience supports the author's general conception of bringing otherwise dry ancient wisdom…"

"Can ancient wisdom be dry?"

"Yes, if it's presented in an overly intellectual manner."

"So, ancient wisdom needs an infusion of emotion?"

"I think so."

"And your own personal experience confirms the author's truth?"

"What does that term mean?"

"What term?"

"The author's truth."

"What does it mean to you?"

"To me it means that the author is expressing her understanding of the subject she has chosen to share with her readers; an understanding she has developed from personal experience, as well as from dedicated study."

"Is that all?"

"Is it possible for her truth to mean more?"

"Yes."

"What?"

"His truth."

"The author is female."

"Yes."

A simple seeker's note to herself

Lesson 33   Thinking back at lesson 33, Spirit didn't seem impressed with my concern about Ancient Wisdom.

"Dry Ancient Wisdom."

"I meant no offence."

"What did you mean?"

"I sincerely meant that ancient wisdom was written and taught away back then, by and for people who lived a much less complicated life than most of us live, now. And, most people were much less educated then, than they are now."

"How would that change wisdom?"

"It wouldn't necessarily change the essence of the wisdom, but it would require that wisdom to be taught in a language and for a people living today, if we're meant to understand it. Also, it seemed to be taught only to a small group of men. Women were, or seemed to be, excluded."

"Would including women change the wisdom?"

"It would certainly seem to require changing the gender specific language."

"Yes."

"Does that mean that you agree with me?"

"Yes."

Closing Comments

Dear Reader,

Perhaps you may have suspected that I wasn't at all as confident of my ability to discuss important life issues with Spirit as I may have seemed to be. I come from that old school style of "fake it until you make it," Much of the time, I pretended to be brave and knowledgeable, even knowing that Spirit would easily see through my pretense. He generously allowed me to play the fool, knowing that I sincerely wanted and needed to learn what He seemed so willing to teach me. I must publicly thank him for his kindness toward me, a simple seeker.

Jean

Printed in the United States
by Baker & Taylor Publisher Services